Sport and My Body

Dancing

Catherine Veitch

www.raintreepublishers.co.uk
Visit our website to find out
more information about
Raintree books.

To order:
☏ Phone +44 (0) 1865 888066
🖷 Fax +44 (0) 1865 314091
🖳 Visit www.raintreepublishers.co.uk

Raintree is an imprint of Capstone Global Library
Limited, a company incorporated in England and Wales
having its registered office at 7 Pilgrim Street, London,
EC4V 6LB – Registered company number: 6695582

"Raintree" is a registered trademark of Pearson
Education Limited, under licence to Capstone Global
Library Limited

Edited by Siân Smith, Rebecca Rissman, and
  Charlotte Guillain
Designed by Joanna Hinton-Malivoire
Picture research by Ruth Blair
Production by Duncan Gilbert
Originated by Chroma Graphics (Overseas) Pte. Ltd
Printed and bound in China by South China Printing
Company Ltd

ISBN 978 1 406 21115 3
13 12 11 10 09
10 9 8 7 6 5 4 3 2 1

British Library Cataloguing in Publication Data
Veitch, Catherine.
  Dancing. -- (Sport and my body)
  1. Dancing--Physiological aspects--Juvenile literature.
  2. Dancing--Social aspects--Juvenile literature.
  I. Title II. Series
  613.7'15-dc22

Acknowledgements
We would like to thank the following for permission
to reproduce photographs: Alamy pp.**7** (© Olivier
Asselin), **18** (© Radius Images), **23** (© Olivier Asselin);
Corbis pp.**15, 4, 21, 23** (Fancy/Veer), **6, 23** (The Irish
Image Collection), **8** (Tim Pannell), **9** (Tom Stewart),
12 (Martin Harvey), **16** (Anna Peisl/zefa), **17** (Gideon
Mendel), **20** (David Ashley); Getty Images pp. **5** (Chris
Jackson), **10** (Jim Esposito/Taxi), **11** (David Handley/
DK), **13** (Paul Chesley), **19** (Frank Siteman), **23** (Paul
Chesley); Photolibrary pp.**14, 23** (Tetra Images);
Shutterstock pp. **22 top left, 22 top right, 22
bottom left, 22 bottom right** (MalibuBooks).

Cover photograph of a boy dancing reproduced with
permission of Punchstock/Photodisc. Back cover images
reproduced with permission of the following: 1. dancer
stretching leg (Photolibrary/© Tetra Images); a pair of
pumps (Shutterstock).

Every effort has been made to contact copyright holders
of material reproduced in this book. Any omissions will
be rectified in subsequent printings if notice is given to
the publishers.

Contents

Some words are shown in bold, **like this**. You can find them in the glossary on page 23.

What is dancing?

When we move to music we are dancing. Dancing is a type of exercise.

We can use dancing to show how we are feeling. We can show if we are feeling happy, sad, scared, or angry.

What types of dance are there?

There are different types of dance around the world. **Irish dancing** comes from Ireland.

People wear special clothes and shoes for different types of dance.

How do I learn to dance?

You can learn to dance anywhere.
You can learn in your home or outside.
All you need is some music or a **beat**.

You can learn special types of dance at a dance class. You need an adult to teach you.

How do I use my legs and feet?

You can use your legs and feet when you jump. You can also use your legs when you turn.

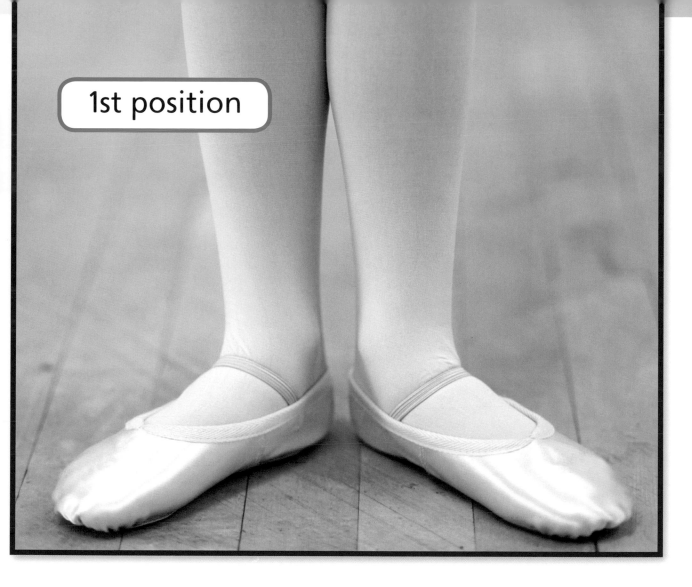

1st position

Where you place your feet is important in dance. In ballet you stand in different **positions**.

How do I use my arms?

You can stretch out your arms to help you **balance**. You can hold your arms in different **positions**.

You can use your arms to show how you feel. You can move your arms slowly or you can move your arms quickly.

What happens to my body when I dance?

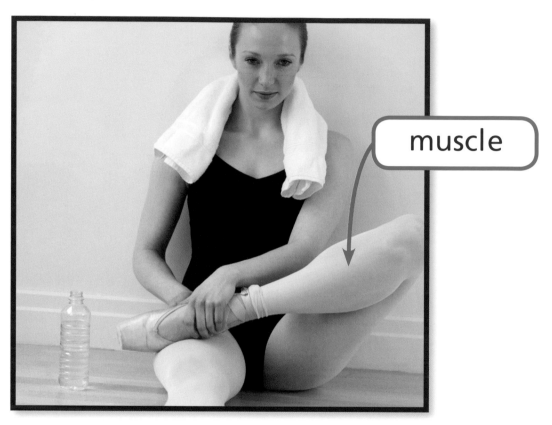

muscle

When you dance your heart will beat faster. Your **muscles** may ache and feel tired.

When you dance you may feel hot and sweaty. You will also feel thirsty.

How does it feel to dance?

You might feel happy when you dance. You may also make good friends as you dance together.

It is fun to watch dance. People like to watch dance together.

Have you ever watched dancers?

How do I stay safe dancing?

muscle

You should always warm up before you dance. Gentle bounces and swinging your arms and legs will warm up your **muscles**.

It is important to listen to your dance teacher. Your teacher will show you how to move safely.

Does dancing make me healthy?

Dancing is good exercise and will help you to keep fit. You should also eat healthy food and drink plenty of water.

To stay healthy you need to get plenty of rest too. Then you can have fun in many different ways.

Dancing shoes

ballet shoes

trainers

pumps

tap shoes

Glossary

 **balance** to keep yourself or an object steady so that it does not fall

 **beat** in music this is a regular sound, sometimes made by a drum. Listening to the beat can help you to keep in time with the music.

 **Irish dancing** traditional type of dance that began in Ireland

 **muscle** part of your body that helps you to move. Exercise can make muscles bigger and stronger.

 **position** place where something is. We put our arms in different positions when we move them around and use them to make different shapes.

Index

Find out more

http://www.dance-kids.org
On this website, you will find lots of games, competitions, and information about dancing.

http://www.childrenandarts.org.uk/events/category/dance
This website lists lots of dance events for children.